GUIDING YOUR CHILD
THROUGH SCHOOL

ARROWS SWIFT & FAR

GUIDING YOUR CHILD THROUGH SCHOOL

Nancy Devlin, PhD

authorHOUSE®

AuthorHouse™
1663 Liberty Drive
Bloomington, IN 47403
www.authorhouse.com
Phone: 1-800-839-8640

Published by AuthorHouse   08/30/2012

ISBN: 978-1-4772-4420-3 (sc)
ISBN: 978-1-4772-4450-0 (e)

Library of Congress Control Number: 2012912629

Any people depicted in stock imagery provided by Thinkstock are models, and such images are being used for illustrative purposes only.
Certain stock imagery © Thinkstock.

This book is printed on acid-free paper.

Because of the dynamic nature of the Internet, any web addresses or links contained in this book may have changed since publication and may no longer be valid. The views expressed in this work are solely those of the author and do not necessarily reflect the views of the publisher, and the publisher hereby disclaims any responsibility for them.

Excerpt from The Prophet by Kahlil Gibran reprinted by permission of Alfred A. Knopf, Inc. Copyright 1923 by Kahlil Gibran and renewed 1951 by Administrators C. T. A. of Kahlil Gibran Estate and Mary G. Gibran.

Additional copies of this book can be requested through the contact form contained on the website and Blog, www.Cassandrasclassroom.com

This book is dedicated to all parents. I regard as parents all you caring people who have accepted the awesome commitment to raise a child to responsible adulthood. You deserve to be loved, cherished and encouraged.

And a woman who held a babe against her bosom said,
Speak to us of Children.

And he said: Your children are not your children
They are the sons and daughters of Life's longing for itself.
They come through you but not from you,
And though they are with you yet they belong not to you.

You may give them your love but not your thoughts,
For they have their own thoughts.
You may house their bodies but not their souls,
For their souls dwell in the house of tomorrow, which you cannot visit, not even in your dreams.
You may strive to be like them, but seek not to make them like you.

For life goes not backward nor tarries with yesterday.
You are the bows from which your children as living arrows are sent forth.
The Archer sees the mark upon the path of the infinite, and He bends you with His might that His arrows may go swift and far.
Let your bending in the Archer's hand be for gladness.
For even as He loves the arrow that flies, so He loves the bow that is stable.

THE PROPHET
Kahlil Gibran

*   *   *

For clarity I have consistently used female pronouns when referring to teachers and male pronouns when referring to students. Our language, at present, offers only cumbersome alternatives to gender-biased pronouns.

*   *   *

CONTENTS

Preface

Never doubt that a small group of thoughtful, committed citizens can change the world. Indeed, it's the only thing that ever has.

Margaret Mead

Your child is going to spend a great part of his life in school. Before he enters school, you are in charge of making all decisions. You can decide whether or not to send him to pre-school programs. You can choose how often to send him, and you can make any changes you feel proper at any time. Suddenly, when your child becomes five, the school system takes over with its many customs, regulations and laws. You now face a system which has been in power for generations. You lose control but still bear primary responsibility for the education of your child.

What can you do? The most important thing you can do is to become informed. That is the goal of this book. To help you to understand the school system so that you can ensure that your child will receive a proper education.

You may never have experienced a good school system yourself. You may not know what the possibilities are, what your rights are or what you can and should expect. You may approach the educational system as the student you once were. Maybe you were reasonably successful at school; maybe not. But in any case, you were taught that the school is the authority, and that you must humbly submit.

Now try to approach the school system as you have learned to approach the health care system. You know how to choose a doctor, a hospital, how to describe symptoms, how to monitor medicines. You keep informed to avoid becoming a victim of the very system that is supposed to be helping you. The same thing should be true of your dealings with the educational system.

You can best help the school system to succeed by being supportive, by encouraging the people in the system and by understanding what schools can and cannot do. It is not enough to complain about what is wrong; you need to know what is right. This means understanding, monitoring, supplementing and, possibly, changing the school system to guarantee that it fulfills its educational mandate.

Our schools have a great deal to offer if you know how to use them well. You are up to the challenge if you have the information needed to deal successfully with the system. When you make decisions about your child, you base them on the information you have at the time. It is important, therefore, for you to acquire the knowledge necessary to make wise and informed decisions. This book is intended to start you on the path to obtaining that knowledge.

Chapter 1

Kindergarten Screening

"It is the highest creatures who take the longest to mature and are the most helpless during their immaturity."

Bernard Shaw

Did you have to take an entrance exam to get into kindergarten? Were your kindergarten days filled with reading, writing, workbooks and finally the taking of a standardized test? Did you ever fail kindergarten?

Sound ridiculous? Well that is a real possibility for some of today's children. They experience a world different from the one you did, for better or for worse.

Understand the Test Results
Learn How Test Results Are Used
Know When to Give Your Child Another Year

Understand the Test Results

The first contact you will have with the school system will be the kindergarten screening tests. These tests usually include the following:

- Free drawing and figure copying,
- Language comprehension and expression,
- Reasoning and counting,
- Balancing and motor coordination.

It helps to keep in mind that these tests are not infallible. They have big uncertainties and measure neither your child's intelligence nor his ability to do appropriate school work.

Remember that there is great variability in the rate of normal development, but all children get there eventually. As long as your child is following a normal sequence of development, he is okay and you are okay. Do not let anybody tell you anything different.

A very discouraged parent reported the following incident involving her son: She knew that he would be one of the youngest in his kindergarten class and that she probably would not send him but give him another year to develop. However, she felt no harm would be done by his taking the screening test. The results might give her some useful information. That did not happen.

After the testing, she and her husband were summoned to school to a meeting. At this meeting, they were given their son's test results in negative terms. Instead of saying sentences like: "He can do 'this' now because he is four and a half," or "He will learn 'that' later because it is an older skill," the officials described their son by pointing out everything he could not do. These parents were crushed, and, tragically lost some level of confidence in themselves and their son. In addition, their child's test results and interpretations by the school system then became part of his permanent school record.

Schools tend to view children in terms of the rate of the "average" child's development. "Average" is a statistical group concept, and it does not allow for the uniqueness of the development of the individual child. As a result, a child can be declared out of step when, in actual fact, the system is out of step with the child.

You can protect your child's self-esteem if you know the normal sequence of physical, intellectual, emotional and social development of children. If the school begins to tell you what your child cannot do, stop them and have them tell you what he can do. You will be able to judge whether what they say is true for your child if you know, understand, and accept the unique rate at which your child develops early childhood skills.

Early Skills

During the first few years of life, a child learns a staggering array of skills. No subsequent stage of life approaches this period in achievement. Here are just some of the skills acquired:

- gross motor skills: crawling, walking, climbing stairs, running, jumping,
- fine motor skills: grasping and manipulating objects, hand-eye coordination,
- cognitive skills: watching, listening, attention span, color recognition, counting, remembering, time sense, relationships,
- communication skills: understanding and speaking language,
- social skills: recognition of and response to himself and others,
- self-help skills: feeding, dressing and washing himself

Within reasonable limits, the sequence of developmental milestones is more important than the age at which each milestone is passed. The time-tables used in most books are merely approximations and there is great variability, which is normal among children. Be alert, however, for any **serious** delays which could be caused by some physical problem. For example, hearing loss could delay communication skills.

Learn How Test Results Are Used

At one time the teaching of reading and writing in kindergarten was not permitted. Now most schools use kindergarten screening tests to determine if children are ready for the predetermined curriculum which includes these subjects. School systems rarely use these test results to plan a curriculum appropriate for the in-coming kindergarten class. Rather, the test results are used to exclude children the system regards as unready for their first school experience.

As a result, some children are declared more ready than others. This can have a devastating effect on you, as parents. For five years you have been very happy watching and helping your child develop. Then he is given a test, usually lasting less than half an hour, and you are led to believe that in some way your child is deficient. He is not as ready as his peers for kindergarten. You can not only lose confidence in yourself as parents; you can also lose confidence in your child.

Remember in this situation that you are your child's advocate and that you know him best. If the school, after less than half an hour of testing, tells you something about your child that you disagree with, trust your own judgment.

Know When To Give Your Child Another Year

Until school systems change, it might be worthwhile for you to consider giving your young son another year before sending him to kindergarten and enrolling him into the system. I say son because at this age boys develop on a different time-table from girls which makes it harder for them to accomplish the goals set for today's kindergartners. Another year might give him enough time to reach the developmental level necessary to score well on readiness tests and to succeed with today's kindergarten program. So many parents of young boys are doing this now that it may force the school system to re-evaluate its kindergarten curriculum. Currently, many children, especially young boys, are given tasks they are not developmentally ready to do. As a result they lose their enthusiasm for learning and begin to have poor self-images and to think of themselves as failures, unable to learn.

Parents of kindergarten children can best help them by acknowledging that all children develop and mature at different rates and the rate of development has nothing to do with intelligence. Parents who attempt to accelerate this rate are doing their children a disservice and frustrating them unnecessarily. Have confidence in your child and his ability to be successful and he will not disappoint you. At the same time, monitor the kindergarten program to be certain that your child is not being stressed by a program which is too far ahead or too far behind his stage of development.

Chapter 2

The First Day At School

"There are few successful adults who were not first successful children."

Perspective
Alexander Chase

There is excitement as well as apprehension in the air at the beginning of any school year. This is especially true for children entering school for the first time and for their parents. Similar feelings can be true for older children entering a new school or simply anticipating contact with new classmates. For many, the transition is smooth and free of anxiety. For others, it is a fearful time.

Some Things Children and Parents Fear
How to Prepare For the First Day
The First Day And After

Some Things Children and Parents Fear

By the time your child is ready to enter school for the first time, he is able to anticipate differences between the familiar, comfortable environment at home and this new, strange place called school. Anticipation of the change to school life can be fearful especially if the child does not know what to expect. Sometimes, older children tease younger ones with horror stories about school.

The kindergartner, new to elementary school, may be afraid that his mother will never find him at the end of the day because the school is so big. Or, he may fear that he will get off of the bus at the wrong stop and be lost forever. Or, he might be afraid he will forget his name and address when the teacher asks him and fail his first school task.

There is a Peanuts cartoon in which Sally comes home from her first day at school and says to her brother, Charlie Brown: "You goofed big brother. You told me to bring a lunch box to school and everybody else brown-bagged it." Charlie Brown's response is: "I can't stand the responsibility." We may all feel that way when even having the wrong lunch box can be viewed as a disaster.

The older child, too, may have anxieties about the first day of a new school year. He may be worried about a new set of classmates or how a new teacher will feel about him. He may fear that they will have no friends or that he will be bullied and cry. He may be unsure that he has the right clothes and fear they will bring him ridicule.

Parents also have fears. They do not know how to protect their children from the hurts they may experience. They fear making wrong decisions because of the conflicting advice they are given on how to help their children. They fear their children will not do well in school and may not be as well prepared as the other students.

How to Prepare For the First Day

The first-day fears of parents and children are real and legitimate. Most resolve themselves in the first few days of school. However, by anticipating them and taking corrective action, the transition can be eased.

For a kindergartner or a child new to a school, it helps if you take him to school before it starts in September. Show your child where you will pick him up. If there is an older sibling in the school, he might go with you to introduce the newcomer to the school. The message to the child is that everyone knows where he is and he will not be forgotten or left alone. If he will be using the bus, show him where it will stop and try to have an adult meet your child at his stop the first week of school.

If your child expresses many concerns and fears about starting school, use reflective listening skills because he may just need a sympathetic ear which gives him the opportunity to resolve his concerns. Do not say that his concerns are baseless. He may never tell you anything again.

Reflective listening requires that you listen to what the child is saying and state back to him your understanding of what he has said. If the child says: "I don't want to go to school. I have no friends there." A reflective response might be. "You feel upset because you are afraid that nobody will like you." This is an open response. It addresses the child's feelings which are very important. It gives him some feedback which tells him that you understand, and it leaves the way open for him to explore solutions.

The First Week And After

Parents very naturally want to know all about their child's school day. Give your child the freedom to choose the things which excite him about this brand new experience. Resist the temptation to go through his school bag. Do not interrogate him about school the minute he gets home. He may be bursting to tell you about the friends he made on the playground or how well he kicked the ball at soccer. Remember that school is an opportunity to learn social and physical skills as well as academic skills. You may cut off that kind of communication if you immediately focus only on academic things.

Suppose that your child comes home from school and asserts that he never wants to go back there again. Suppose he claims to be sick, and you know that this is untrue. In the past, this was called "school-phobia," and the conventional wisdom was to insist that the child return no matter what his objections. In today's world, this may be a mistake. Children's concerns should be taken seriously. Whether the underlying problem is trivial or serious, it is very real for the child. Many problems do not truly threaten your child's safety, but some do and you should be alert for them.

Ask why he does not want to go to school. You and he may be able to solve the problem quickly once you know what it is. If your child does not know or is unwilling to tell you the nature of his problem, play detective. Find out what is wrong and take appropriate action. Learn how things look from your child's viewpoint. This may require that you go with him to school and spend some time there.

If your child walks to school, go with him along his usual route. Discuss with him the things you see and be alert to his reactions to them. Sometimes a child has to pass a house where a particularly nasty dog lives, and he is frightened every day. Or he may regularly meet a group of older children who frighten him.

At school, ask permission to spend time in his classroom, lunchroom and playground. If you have time, you might volunteer to go on the first class trip or to become the "room parent." Your most important goal is find out if your child's world is unsafe. If there is nothing which really threatens his safety, look for other causes for his school refusal.

One child, after a week at school, claimed to be sick. Two days at home convinced his mother that he was using this as an excuse not to go to school. By detective work she and the teacher learned that her son feared using the lavatory which was in the classroom. The door had no lock and he envisioned another student walking in while he was having a bowel movement. The solution was to give him permission to use the boys' room in the hall which had locks on the individual stalls. This solution satisfied the child and he returned to school.

A mother came to see me because she was having difficulty every morning getting her son to go to school. After meeting with the teacher, the mother and the child, I developed a hypothesis. I suggested to the boy that he invite his mother to lunch at school, and he did. On the day of the lunch, he appeared at my office and asked, "Did you call her?" "Does she know where to go?" "You'd better call her, or she'll get lost." This confirmed my hypothesis. The boy felt that his mother was unable to function without his help. Apparently the mother said sentences like, "I don't know how I'll get through the day." "Everything's a mess." Since the boy was a concrete thinker, he took what she said literally and wanted to be home to help her get through the day. The solution was the luncheon visits. Once he became convinced that she was able to continue through the rest of the day, his fears were eased.

Another very overweight boy refused to go to middle school. Detective work revealed that the required gym shorts were too small for him and the other children made fun of him. The solution was to allow him to wear properly sized sweat pants in gym. He agreed to return to school and to gym.

While these solutions seem simple and obvious, it is important that they be found quickly. The longer the child's aversion to school persists, the more damage is done.

Chapter 3

Your First Meeting with the Teacher

"Instruction begins when you, the teacher, learn from the learner, put yourself in his place so that you may understand what he learns, and the way he understands it."

The Journals
Soren Kierkegaard, 1854

Each year in school, your child is introduced to a teacher with whom he will spend the next ten months. You can and should meet this new teacher early in the school year to help her to learn about your child. Describe your child in positive terms so that the teacher is given enough information to plan appropriately for a successful year. In order to do this, you must understand your child. You need to know his temperament, his learning style, his hobbies and his interests.

Initiate a Meeting
Describe Your Child In Positive Terms
Monitor and Supplement Your Child's Program

Initiate a Meeting

Good school systems encourage parents to discuss their concerns with teachers and other school officials. You can and should initiate a conference early in the school year for any child, but especially if you have a child who always seems to be misunderstood or who has difficulty adjusting to the school routine. These are usually the children described as: "Marching to a Different Drummer."

> The verb "to educate" means "to lead", "to draw out", "to develop." It does not imply changing children into something they are not. In its highest sense, education is to take children as they are with their individual inclinations, strengths and preferences and to draw out and to develop their best qualities. Each child is unique and should be treated uniquely.

> The same can be said for teachers. Each teacher is unique with different teaching and learning styles and strengths. When teachers and students understand, accept and rejoice in each other's differences, true learning takes place.

Some parents take a "wait and see" attitude hoping things will be different this time around. The best strategy is to take action first. A conference is your opportunity to enlist the cooperation of the teacher by creating for your child a school environment which will enhance learning and self-esteem. It is also an opportunity for you to meet the teacher in order to understand her unique temperament, teaching style, strengths and weaknesses.

Describe Your Child In Positive Terms

When you describe your child, do so in **concrete, positive** terms. The purpose of this description is not to have the teacher change your child but to have her understand and accept him as he is. Do not talk about what he cannot do; rather describe what he **can** do, what his needs are, and how he can be helped to learn. To do this well you will need to know your child, his temperament and his learning style.

Some parents are surprised to learn that they do not know as much about their child as they thought they did.

When asked, one parent admitted that she found it difficult to describe her child's likes and dislikes. She was not sure what he would do in his spare time because he had no spare time. He had piano lessons on Monday, soccer on Tuesday, French on Wednesday, soccer again on Thursday and so on through the week. All activities structured by other people. Left to himself, what would he do? He had no time for dreaming or developing his unique personality.

In order to be able to describe your child to his teacher, you need to take the time to know him. You can learn by observing your child over a period time to discover whether he is an auditory or visual learner, sequential or systematic learner, or what is sometimes termed "right-brained" or "left-brained" learner. By observation, you can also learn about his temperament: how he perceives the world and processes information and how he relates to other people and approaches new tasks.

You might start by observing if your child learns best by the use of concrete objects like pictures and models which help him to visualize and to understand the whole concept. Or does he do better when the concept is broken down into a step-by-step, linear explanation with verbal cues. The latter type of learning is thought to be a function of the left side of the brain, and most teaching and testing in school is geared to this type of learning. The "right-brained" child, who learns through spatial relationships and who sees things simultaneously as a whole, may be at a disadvantage unless the teacher knows and accommodates to his style.

Watch to see how your child behaves. Is he very active? Does he need to touch and to manipulate objects in order to learn? Does he work best in small groups? Does he get distracted when there is too much activity and too many choices? Does he have a short attention span? Does he learn best when he can work for a short period of time and then take some kind of break? Does he like to work alone on one project for long periods without interruption?

Can you describe your child in any of these ways?

"He seems to understand everything but sometimes forgets the little details."

"He loses things and has so many interests he tends to go from one thing to another."

"He likes to know exactly what is expected of him and can memorize quickly."

All of these sentences describe how your child perceives and processes information and give you insights into his temperament.

No one way of learning is better than another, they are just different. Children learn best using their preferred mode of learning. If your child is constantly thwarted from working with his preferred style, he may not learn as well or as easily as he should. He may also feel that there is something wrong with him because he thinks and acts differently from the rest of the class. These feelings may produce rebellious behavior or cause him to stop trying. You can prevent this from happening to your child not only by understanding and accepting his style but also by encouraging others in his world to do the same.

The first meeting with the teacher is a "get-acquainted" session. You have come to describe your child and to hear the teacher's thoughts on education and children. Most teachers are interested in knowing about their students, especially if you can be very concrete in your descriptions and suggestions for what works best. You seek to understand what your child will experience in that classroom and how compatible the teacher's style is with your child's needs. You know your child best and do not be afraid to share this understanding with the teacher and to correct any misconceptions she may have.

Monitor and Supplement Your Child's Program

After your meeting with the teacher, you may find that the information you gave is not being incorporated into a meaningful program for your child. When that happens and you feel another meeting with the teacher will not bring about any changes, it may be time to supplement the school program.

If your child works best using concrete objects and the teacher only uses workbook pages, then at home you should provide opportunities to be concrete. Here are some examples.

- Take your child shopping and have him help you figure out how much things cost and use real money to pay for them.
- Build something together, perhaps a small cabinet or a birdhouse. Have him sketch out a design, choose sizes and shapes, figure out dimensions, purchase the materials and build it.
- Design your own field trips. Take him to the antiquities museum when the topic is ancient civilizations, to the county courthouse when the topic is civics, to the zoo or aquarium when the topic is biology.

If most of the school time is spent sitting in seats and being inactive, then when your child comes home provide opportunities for him to use his body. If your child likes quiet but is in a noisy classroom, provide quiet time for him to work on his own projects at home.

If your child likes to solve problems and to use logic, but the teacher emphasizes rote learning, encourage him to ask questions at home. Expose him to challenges to his thinking and reasoning. Try lots of things and find out which catch his interest. Here are some possibilities.

- "Brain Twister" books with puzzles which require reasoning to solve.
- Chess, bridge and other games in which thinking, planning and logic play a major role.
- At an appropriate age, computer programs which require mathematical and logical reasoning.

If the teacher spends more time on science than literature, then you can read poems and fantasy stories at home. If there is little time given to science, then you can spend more time at the science or "hands-on" museums that year.

If your child is not successful in any of the structured school-type activities, then it is very important that you provide an opportunity for him to be successful outside of the school. Try activities like model-building, playing a musical instrument, photography, sports, art or theater.

School systems and individual teachers vary widely in their approach to educating children. Each school year is different for your child. You need to monitor his progress constantly in order to get the best from the school, and, whenever necessary, to supplement the school's program.

A classification of psychological types developed by Carl Jung, a Swiss psychiatrist can be a tool to determine learning styles. The classifications attempt to describe how people perceive and judge the world and the relative emphasis they place on their interior and exterior lives.

In perceiving the world, **sensing** people rely mostly on their five senses. They look at the world in terms of what they can see, touch, hear, taste and smell. Students and teachers who prefer sensing stress fact over theory and reality over imagination.

Other people use **intuition** when perceiving the world. They go beyond the observable facts to possibilities, meanings and relationships. Students and teachers who use intuition favor abstraction and symbolic reasoning.

Some people prefer making judgments and coming to decisions objectively and impersonally and are called **thinking**. Students and teachers who prefer thinking analyze the facts.

People with a **feeling** style have a preference for making judgments subjectively and personally. Students and teachers who prefer feeling weigh values and are concerned about how others feel.

Extroverts like to talk and be with people, and they enjoy projects that require working in groups. **Introverts**. On the other hand, tend to keep their feelings to themselves. They enjoy privacy and need quiet time to do their best work.

Chapter 4

Homework

"A man ought to read just as inclination leads him; for what he reads as a task will do him little good."

Samuel Johnson

Did you hate homework when you were in school? Did it make you a better person? How are you going to deal with your child's homework assignments?

Homework has the potential for bringing your family together or disrupting it. Since most school systems mandate nightly homework assignments beginning with first grade, it behooves you to use this activity well in order to help your child grow as a learner.

Understand the Goals and Limits of Homework
Observe How Your Child Deals with Homework
Request More Creative Assignments
Be Alert For Problems
Do Not Let Homework Disrupt Your Family

Understand the Goals and Limits of Homework

Homework, along with its role in the learning process, is an important topic for discussion by school officials, parents and students early in the school year. Homework will enhance the learning process only if its purpose is clearly understood and its guidelines agreed upon. It should be an integral part of the curriculum, not something added on in order to discipline the child.

Some schools view homework as a way to toughen the student, to prepare him to face the "real world." Sometimes homework is used as a punitive exercise unrelated to the curriculum. The purpose of homework, in this view, is disciplinary. Disciplining the mind is important, but it cannot be accomplished by giving poorly designed homework assignments. It may have the opposite effect. While you may be able to force children to do homework now, the negative backlash may produce adults who never want to open another book or to learn another thing.

The ideal result of homework should be an eagerness to pursue something independently without the constraints of a school building. In the end, homework is voluntary. It should not be something the school demands, with noncompliance punished by a poor final grade. Instead, it should be something that enhances classroom learning. The best assignments are those which your child can understand, which prepare him for class work and which encourage him to use the tools of learning he acquired in school.

There are ways to do this. Many teachers use reading assignments at home to prepare students for topics to be discussed in class. If your child comes to class with questions that he has developed from the reading, then the assignment has been successful. You, as parents, do not need to insist that he know all of the answers but should encourage his inquisitiveness.

Homework can be used to reinforce skills through practice and drill. Examples are arithmetic and spelling. Children vary greatly in their response to this type of activity. Some acquire a skill only after many repetitions, while others make it their own effortlessly. Encourage your school to be flexible in using these drills as homework. If your child has the skill, boring and repetitious assignments can only sour his attitude toward learning. Ask for alternatives more appropriate to his style.

The best assignments are those in which your child brings home work on concepts he has learned and mastered in school that allow him to demonstrate to you how much he knows. He can glow in the light of your approval. These types of assignments also give you an opportunity to get to know what your child is being taught and is learning in school day by day. One good assignment is for your young child to bring home a book he has successfully learned to read in school to read to you. Assignments in which children constantly fail in front of their parents are to be avoided. If this is happening to your child, go to school quickly and negotiate other assignments for him. A poor self-esteem as a learner is very damaging to young children.

Observe How Your Child Deals With Homework

Homework assignments which take into account the needs of the individual students are helpful. Some children need a great deal of reinforcement before they truly understand a new concept. This reinforcement can be done at home. Other children take longer to finish a classroom assignment, and, rather than miss something else in class, can finish the assignment at home. Some children love to do homework assignments and will spend many happy hours working on them. Others get very upset about doing twenty problems when they already understand the concept. Some children get confused by homework assignments and make so many mistakes that they have to be retaught the concept. Some children are perfectionists and spend two hours on a half-hour task. Others find it hard enough to sit still in school all day and find it even harder to sit still doing homework.

You should know which of these styles fit your child and act accordingly. It helps to describe your child's style to the teacher and, with your child participating, negotiate for the appropriate homework assignments.

Request More Creative Assignments

At home, parents have an advantage the schools lack. Schools are constrained by the building and the numbers of children in the class. This is why workbooks are used and photocopy sheets are given to children. To send home worksheets for children to do in isolation wastes the opportunity for creative use of the world outside of the school building.

With some thought, parents and teachers could come up with creative homework assignments that would use the tools of learning. Examples are: reading the newspaper critically and writing a comment on what was read, writing a critique on a television program, interviewing neighbors with different occupations on how they prepared themselves for their careers, writing letters to pen pals, playing family card games and doing puzzles, keeping track of the weather and weather predictions. The advantage of these types of assignments is that children are introduced to the concept of learning as a lifelong activity and not something that only happens in a school building with a teacher prompting.

Be Alert For Problems

School systems tend to leave it up to the individual teachers to incorporate homework into their programs. Some teachers never correct homework or correct it in such a way that the child becomes confused.

One first grade student had his corrected math homework sheet sent home with one answer circled in red because he had written the number 7 backwards. The student concluded that 4 + 3 does not equal 7.

You may need to check how the teacher grades your child's homework. Good work should be recognized explicitly, not just ignored. The best grading marks what the child did right rather than what he did wrong. When something is marked incorrect, the teacher should provide some guidance about what is correct. The grading should enhance, not diminish, your child's learning and self-confidence.

School Systems vary greatly on how much time they feel should be spent on homework. In Houston, concerned parents insisted that the school system limit homework to forty-five minutes a day for young children. Before this limit was set, some first graders were spending ninety minutes a day on homework. For some children, especially those with learning problems, an assignment which seemed short by the teacher's standards could be very long and frustrating for the child.

It helps if parents and teachers decide early in the school year the length of time the children should be spending on homework. The time spent should vary according to the grade level. If your child is spending an inordinate amount of time and becoming very upset, let the teacher know. An agreement should be reached about how much time is reasonable. You, the parent can confirm that your child did, in fact, spend the agreed amount of time and he should be permitted to stop, without penalty, whether the assignment is completed or not. Remember, you are your child's advocate.

Poorly conceived homework is a grave error on the part of the school because the potential is great for damaging the learning process and for creating disharmony in homes already under stress. An enthusiastic learner can quickly become an indifferent one if assignments are boring, and repetitious. Overlong assignments, not conducive to learning, can use up valuable time which children could be spending more profitably on their own creative ideas and projects. Many parents are often confused about homework and its value but feel that as good parents they should insist that their children complete these assignments no matter what. The way is paved for power struggles and anger. It can create rebellious behavior in children who fight their parents about doing the assignment.

Do Not Let Homework Disrupt Your Family

Some parents feel personally responsible when children do not do their homework. This feeling is reinforced by teachers who complain to parents when the homework is not done rather than discussing the problem with the student. It is important for parents and teachers to remember that homework is the child's responsibility. Parents can provide a quiet place for their child to work, and they can provide assistance, support and encouragement, but it is not their homework. It is their child's.

A parent's attempts to change a child's homework habits often impair the child's academic performance thus inhibiting learning. Some children do not respond well to a parent's attempt to help them and everybody winds up in a screaming match. Many times a parent's efforts are met with the sentence, "But that's not the way my teacher does it." For some teenagers, not doing homework is their only way of showing independence.

The potential for dissension is great if your child brings home an assignment involving a concept totally new and unfamiliar to him, one which has not yet been taught in school. In trying to teach him the concept, you can get frustrated and lose faith in your child as a learner because he does not understand as quickly or as well as you think he should. The child also loses faith in himself and now has the added fear that he will lose your love. This can be very damaging to the child's self-image and could affect his future learning. If your child is struggling with new, unfamiliar concepts, tell the teacher what is happening at home and enlist her support to bring about a change.

One suggestion for avoiding dissension over homework is to have a time after dinner reserved for quiet, mental activity for the whole family, with the TV off. This avoids sending one child off to his room to do his homework while the rest of the family is making noise and apparently enjoying watching TV. You cannot use a "do as I say not as I do" attitude toward learning, especially learning to enjoy reading and other mental pursuits. Your children should have visible evidence that you value these activities.

It is very important for adults to remember that the purpose of educating children is to give them the tools to be lifelong learners. Any school or home activity which has the opposite effect, should be carefully scrutinized, evaluated and changed when necessary.

Chapter 5

Report Cards

"A failure is not always a mistake; it may simply be the best one can do under the circumstances. The real mistake is to stop trying."

B. F. Skinner

What does your child do in school every day? What are his favorite subjects? How is he doing and does he enjoy it?

You need to know how well your child is doing in school. The school's method of reporting to you and your reaction to these reports should be supportive and encouraging to the child. Poor reporting techniques and adverse reaction of parents to negative reports can deeply damage a child's attitude toward learning.

Compliment Good Grades Rather Than Complain About Poor Grades
Emphasize Learning Rather Than Grades
Be an Advocate for Good Reporting Techniques

Compliment Good Grades Rather Than Complain About Poor Grades

Report cards can be an effective and constructive channel for communication between schools and parents. Ideally, a report card will emphasize a child's successes, and it will characterize his weaker areas not as failures on the part of the child, but as areas where the school and student will seek to do better. A growing trend is to have a portfolio for each child containing examples of his work.

Children are concrete thinkers, and grades can be confusing to them because they are abstract. When schools report what children have done wrong rather than what they have done right, children become fearful of making mistakes and avoid risks. Over concern with mistakes often causes children to make more rather than fewer mistakes and, instead of learning from their mistakes, they become discouraged. This is especially true of students who are fiercely competitive, or who set unrealistically high standards for themselves. If their excessive ambition is the result of basic inferiority feelings, then these feelings are reinforced when they make mistakes and fail to get an "A" for their work.

One kindergartner brought home his first attempt at printing the letter "a". The teacher wrote at the top of the paper, "Be Neater". Since the child could not read, he did not know what he had done wrong. He only knew the teacher was not pleased with his work. The teacher became concerned when she noticed he never took home another paper. He threw them in the basket. The teacher realized that it would have been more useful to report to the child what he had done right. She could have looked at the paper of "a's" and pointed out those that were formed correctly and asked him to make more like those.

Since it takes time and repeated mistakes to learn a new skill, schools might be more helpful to students if they encouraged the effort, graded the final product, and not the intermediate steps.

Emphasize Learning Rather Than Grades

The best motivation for learning is the pleasure in doing it. This motivation begins in elementary school and is perpetuated by parents' attitude. Since our grading system is largely based on comparing students to some standard, most of the students' motivation is to get a good grade. Many students will not take a course which offers enjoyment or challenge if they fear a mediocre grade in the course. Why take calculus and risk getting a "B" when you can take rudimentary math and be assured of an "A"? They are working for the grade not the knowledge.

You can counteract this attitude by asking your child what he learned or how he enjoyed school rather than questioning why he got a "B" rather than an "A". Try inquiring what kind of questions he asked in school that day. Children who feel pressured to get top grades sometimes will copy from others or will change their answers in an effort to cover up mistakes. Many children will deny ignorance. This can deprive them of instruction they need in order to take the next step in learning, and sabotage their future learning. They have not developed the courage to be imperfect. Children need to learn that while improvement is always possible, perfection never is. You can help your child with this by admitting that you, too, make mistakes. You can create an atmosphere in your home where it is safe to make mistakes.

Be an Advocate for Good Reporting Techniques

When your child brings home a report card which contains only uncommented grades, you learn very little from it. The only information such report cards really contain is how your child is doing relative to some often unspecified standard.

Such a report is not helpful to your child, especially when its interpretation is obscure to him. It is some secret shared only by adults. This seems strange since it is the child's learning that is being evaluated and the child is the most important person in the process. He is ultimately the one who will decide for himself whether he will or will not learn. You need to make sure that he gets clear and encouraging information. It is important that you be aware of your child's progress in school in order to encourage him, and to monitor the school program in order to change it or to supplement it when necessary.

Uncommented letter grades give you no objective information about how your child is progressing in his skills. You need this information in order to monitor his program especially in the critical skill of reading. You need to know your child's progress in reading. Do not wait an entire year to detect a problem. Interim report cards should give you the reading levels of the books he is using. If your child does not show progress in reading, it is time to request a different program for him.

One alert parent discovered that her son's reading level was not improving. She learned that, in her school system, there was just one reading program for the whole school. Her son, who had hearing problems as a baby, was just not learning from this system. The school informed the parent that the only way her child could get another reading program was for him to be classified handicapped. After talking to other parents, this mother found that other children were also not learning from this program. The parents took action together, and got another reading program added to the curriculum.

You should make the assumption that your child can learn to read if taught correctly. As your child advances in school, it becomes more and more difficult for him to catch up after a critical skill has been poorly taught. In middle school, there no longer are different reading groups for different reading levels. All children are given the same books. By the time your child reaches middle school, he should be at or very close to grade level in reading.

Ideally, there should be another type of report card to help you to monitor your child's progress better. This type of reporting would be more objective and it would avoid comparisons with other children. It would inform you of your individual child's program and progress. It would present your child's reading and math levels and the textbooks currently being used. It would describe how well he uses the English language in speech and writing. It would report his capacity for higher level thinking, for example, how he integrates what he learned about science into a discussion of its effect on history. Whenever appropriate, a narrative portion of this "ideal" report would make mention of his social skills and learning style. A report like this does not have to be long or burdensome to the teacher. A few short phrases can be very revealing and helpful to you.

Learning should be a pleasant, personal, and rewarding experience for children and for their parents. You have a responsibility as parents to be well-informed so that this is the kind of atmosphere for learning your child experiences. If the school's reporting techniques damage this atmosphere, let the school know that you disagree and would be willing to negotiate another way of reporting for your child. Most schools' reporting techniques are based on their interpretation of parents' wishes. Knowing that parents want something different may help schools improve.

Chapter 6

Parent-Teacher Conferences

Man's inability to communicate is a result of his failure to listen effectively, skillfully, and with understanding to another person.

Carl Rogers

Early in the school year, you met with the teacher to tell her what you know about your child. Now, later in the year, conference time has come, and it is the teacher's turn to tell you what she has learned about him. It is an evening with lines of anxious adults waiting for the parent-teacher conference. Are you ready for it? Do you know how to use it to your child's advantage?

Have Your Child Participate In the Conference
In Advance, Agree On the Agenda and Participants
Be Encouraging, Positive and Concrete
At The Conclusion, Summarize the Results

Have Your Child Participate In the Conference

Parent-teacher conferences initiated by the school are a very useful means of communication. This best occurs in an atmosphere of cooperation. When parents or teachers find conferences unpleasant or unproductive, it is time for all of them to change the atmosphere. Both groups need to work cooperatively if the student is to benefit. These conferences are even better when they are made into parent-teacher-student conferences.

Students should be part of all discussions because, in the final analysis, they are the ones in charge of their own learning. Teachers can teach, and parents can support, but if the students decide not to learn, for whatever reason, there is not much adults can do about it. Learning is not a passive activity. Students must conquer the material and make it their own.

The first thing the teacher can do to involve your child is to tell him before the parent-teacher-student conference what she plans to tell you. Your child should be given the opportunity to react either positively or negatively. In principle, what the teacher tells him should not come as a surprise. Students should know how they stand academically.

By being present at the meeting, your child gets all of the information first-hand. This also gives his teacher the opportunity to observe how he responds to you, his parent, in this situation. In turn, it helps you to learn how the teacher and your child respond to each other. If he is not involved in the conference, the teacher reports to you how your child behaves, which may or may not be the whole story, and you must report to your child what the teacher said, which also may suffer in translation. No student is too young for this. I have participated in very successful conferences with parents, teachers and first-grade students.

In Advance, Agree On the Agenda and Participants

Prior to the meeting, you and the school should agree on its time, agenda and participants. If you want a specialist such as the remedial reading teacher at the conference, that request should be made prior to the conference. If the teacher is going to have a school psychologist, social worker, learning consultant or any other member of the Child Study Team at the conference, you should know this.

If the stated purpose of the meeting is to discuss your child's academic program and progress, you should request that the teacher be prepared with samples of his work and a summary of his progress. This summary should be written if at all possible. The summary should include not only areas of concern but also areas of strength. Above all it should be encouraging, not discouraging. All adults at the conference should protect the student's self-esteem and nobody should be permitted verbally to attack the student whether he is present or not.

The purpose of conferences is for all participants to communicate effectively with each other about your child for his benefit. A successful conference involves a variety of useful skills: mediation, listening and communication. Your child can learn much from seeing these skills modeled at such a conference. If you feel insecure in any of these skills, you should seek to improve them.

It helps if you come to the conference with some questions jotted down so that the discussion can be kept directed to its intended task. It is important for you to ensure that your agenda items are addressed as well as the teacher's. Discuss this with your child in advance so that his concerns are also on the agenda. Always remember that you are your child's advocate not his adversary.

Be Encouraging, Positive and Concrete

Nobody should be permitted to label the student or speak negatively about him. If a teacher says that your child is just lazy and does not put forth any effort, it is up to you to challenge this statement and to ask for clarification or concrete examples. Such a statement is too abstract and gives no useful information. It is much more helpful if the teacher says something like, "John does not hand in his homework two of the five times during the week. Thus, he is not ready to participate in the classroom lesson on those days. This is why he is having trouble learning." This is the kind of concrete information that all parties can understand. It allows everyone involved to explore the problem and to suggest solutions.

Whenever you do not understand what is being said, or disagree with a statement, feel free to interrupt and ask for clarification or correction. This is especially true if school officials resort to incomprehensible educational jargon. **Never be embarrassed to ask that something be restated in everyday language.** If the parties in a conference consistently have difficulty in understanding each other, it sometimes helps to have an objective party present to facilitate communication.

At The Conclusion, Summarize the Results

If there are problem areas, positive solutions should have been recommended and a plan of action agreed upon. Each person should summarize his or her understanding of what conclusions have been reached and who is responsible for any action to be taken. Follow-up conferences may be agreed upon with the consent of all involved. If you and the teacher feel that a topic different from the original agenda has come up, agree to pursue it at another time.

All participants have an obligation to be constructive and positive in their approach. At the end of the conference, everyone should feel encouraged and have a sense all are working together toward achievable, beneficial goals.

Courtesy demands that you respect time schedules. Most teachers work on a tight schedule and conferences which go overtime delay waiting parents. Adults should always take the opportunity to model cooperative behavior by concluding conferences on schedule.

Chapter 7

Cumulative Folders and Test Scores

"He had bought a large map representing the sea.
Without the least vestige of land;
And the crew were much pleased when they found it to be
A map they could all understand."

The Hunting of the Snark
Lewis Carroll

Most institutions keep files on their members. In school systems, these files are called cumulative record folders. Do you know that there is one for your child? Do you know what is in it? You should and it is your right to know.

Achievement Test Results
Intelligence Test Results
Comments by Teachers and Other School Officials
Problems with Evaluation Systems

Achievement Test Results

The first time you may become aware of the fact that the school has a cumulative record folder on your child is when you are given a report of standardized test scores. Most schools give these tests to children at the end of each grade. The scores are usually added to your child's cumulative folder in the form of strips of numbers for each grade in school. Some schools include IQ scores which are determined by means of pencil and paper group tests. In addition to the scores, schools may include a computer printout which separates the questions into categories indicating your child's scores in different areas.

You should understand the strengths and weaknesses of standardized tests and how schools use the scores. These tests originally were intended to permit school districts and state governments to evaluate whether or not, on average, their student population was learning and reaching the district goals.

Many school systems, with the encouragement of test publishers, now put scores to other uses which were not part of the original intent. The test results are often used to judge the individual child's progress even though they are not standardized for that purpose.

Test results are also used to judge the teacher's competence. As a result, many teachers ignore the curriculum goals established by the school and teach to the test. In these cases, the test is no longer a tool for the school to evaluate its program, it now *is* the program. You need to know what use the school is making of these test results and how this affects your child's program and progress. You also need to know what the scores mean.

Interpreting Test Scores

There are several possible ways of reporting the results to you. One is percentiles. This score ranges from a low of 1 to a high of 99. If your child scores at the 75th percentile, that means that 75 percent of the children taking this test performed below your child and 25 percent scored higher. Another way is to report grade equivalent scores. In this score, the school year is divided into 10 months and the score is expressed in terms of a decimal number with the grade before the decimal point and the number of months in that grade after it. For example. 7.8 refers to the eighth month (April) in the seventh grade. This type of scoring sometimes gives interesting results. A child in the fifth grade can get a seventh grade score in math. This does not necessarily mean he can do seventh grade math, it means he scored better than the other fifth graders taking the test. The test is only testing fifth grade math and usually does not include questions at the seventh grade level.

If you look at your child's test scores over several grades and see great fluctuations, be sure you take a look at the name of the test that is being recorded. Tests from different companies and even different tests from the same company are not always comparable. For example, primary grade tests are usually for grades first to third. The test then switches to the intermediate level at grade four. As a result, there will be a difference in scores between grades three and four. There are also statistical fluctuations in all test scores due to errors of measurement.

It is very important for you to know not only how the school interprets these scores but also what use is made of these interpretations. The computer printout of standardized test scores is only useful as a screening device to indicate a possible problem area. It is based on too little data to say with certainty that a problem exists and, if so, to identify it. If your child, for example, shows a drop in reading comprehension, you might ask if the school is going to give him a diagnostic test to determine if there is a real problem. Diagnostic tests and tests of hearing and vision give more data and help to pinpoint specific areas of difficulty.

If the school, on the basis of group end-of-year achievement tests, tells you that your child's performance is deficient in some way, you should ask a number of questions. "What further testing will be done to verify and pinpoint the problem?" "What program do you plan for my child in order to help him to learn better and possibly to improve his scores?" In other words, insist that the test scores be used as tools for planning

your child's program and not merely as a statement that your child is deficient in some way.

If you doubt the validity of the scores for a particular year, ask that they be deleted from the folder. You do not need to insist on retesting. It is not very useful to subject the child to the same test again. Another kind of test, possibly one without paper and pencil, might be more revealing, especially for the child who does not test well. Some children fill in the computer-graded answer sheet incorrectly, some get distracted and lose their place, and some just freeze up. Retesting them on the same type of test will not help such problems and it does children a disservice.

Different Kinds of Intelligence

Common sense tells us and research has shown that the human mind is far more complex than data recorded in a cumulative folder. The little we do know indicates that the potential power of the brain is being used minimally at the present time. We do not even know how to define intelligence. Dr. Howard Gardner from Harvard identifies seven different kinds of intelligence:

- logical-mathematical,
- musical,
- bodily-kinesthetic,
- linguistic,
- spatial,
- interpersonal,
- intrapersonal.

How can test publishers and school systems begin to imagine that a single score can be attributed to these complex and multi-dimensional aspects of the human being?

Intelligence Test Results

IQ scores, especially those arrived at by paper-and-pencil tests, should not be in your child's cumulative folders. Such a score is not a measure of your child's native intelligence. At best, the tests measure how well your child filled in the spaces on that particular test in relation to how other children filled in the spaces. A poor test score can be very damaging to a child's future learning especially since it is not infallible, can vary over subsequent testings, and is sensitive to the child's behavior and feelings at the time of testing.

School districts that buy into the publisher's extravagant claims by making these scores part of a child's permanent record, are doing a disservice to its children. Schools should not perpetuate the myth that short answer, fill-in-the-blank or mark-the-right-space tests tell you what your child is capable of accomplishing.

Comments by Teachers and Other School Officials

You should know what is in your child's cumulative folder. It is your right, and your child's right, to know. It is helpful to view the folders during transition points: moving on to middle school and high school. **If you feel the comments do not describe your child in encouraging and objective terms, challenge them. Ask that they either be revised or deleted.**

It is interesting to see what teachers choose to say about a child. Most of the comments tell you more about the teacher than the child. Some teachers consistently write only about the students' intellectual levels, comparing them to others. Some feel that comments on the students' social development are most useful. Other teachers write more about their opinion of the parents than they do about the students.

The most useful comments, however, are those which describe your child in behavioral terms without making judgments or attaching labels. (Chapter 8 discusses labeling.)

Labeling children is not necessary and has the potential for harm. Labels give no useful information because they are too abstract. Instead, ask that your child be described in behavioral terms. Ask that the teacher describe what actually is happening, what he learned and which learning techniques worked. Here are examples:

"He knows most of his history facts, but needs extra time to finish the test and does not do well on timed tests."

"His verbal skills are good, but he has difficulty with numbers."

"He learns well in class discussions, but not as well with written assignments.

Some cumulative records are more noteworthy for the things that are left out of them rather than the things that are left in, such things as positive statements about your child's learning style, temperament, and accomplishments. You should request additions to the folder that would help the next teacher understand and plan for your child by building on his strengths.

Problems with Evaluation Systems

The basic problem with testing and evaluation systems is not only their limited accuracy but also their limited scope. They test only a subset of the full range of human capabilities. School systems place unwarranted faith in these tests. They make judgments and plan programs based on test scores. They erroneously believe that the scores can tell them what a child is capable of accomplishing. Further, they tailor their programs to the narrow set of skills addressed in the tests.

Children live up or down to our best and worst expectations. Research has shown that, when teachers do not expect much from students, that is what they get—not much. The opposite is also true. In one study, teachers were told that twenty percent of their students showed unusual potential for intellectual growth. The names of these twenty percent were chosen at random. Eight months later, these children showed significantly greater gains in IQ than did the remaining children who had not been singled out for the teachers' attention. The authors note that the change in the teachers' expectations regarding the intellectual performance of these allegedly special children had led to an actual change in their intellectual performance.

The 1988 film "Stand and Deliver" was based on a true story. It was assumed that students from a low socio-economic neighborhood could not learn calculus. One splendid teacher refused to accept that judgment. His students learned calculus and astounded the school and testing services by performing far beyond everyone's expectations for this group. At first the testing service suspected cheating because they believed more in their statistics than in the students. They insisted on a re-test, and the students proved that they understood calculus.

One of the worst fallouts from putting individual test scores in cumulative folders is that the school uses them to label children as underachievers or overachievers based on IQ scores. When a child does better or worse academically than the IQ report indicates, it is assumed that the child has done something unexpected. It is amazing that nobody calls into question the validity of the IQ score on which all of these judgments are made. The fact that the scores are never doubted gives an indication of the power these numbers have achieved in peoples' minds.

Remember that for your child the sky is the limit, given the right program and proper motivation. Anything the school does which interferes with his achieving his best should be challenged by you and alternatives offered. You are your child's advocate—the one who gives him unconditional love and support.

Chapter 8

Labeling Children

"Alpha children wear grey. They work much harder than we do, because they're so frightfully clever. I'm really awfully glad I'm a Beta, because I don't work so hard. And then we are much better than the Gammas and Deltas. Gammas are stupid."

Brave New World
Aldous Huxley

"Nothing you become will disappoint me; I have no preconception that I'd like to see you be or do. I have no desire to foresee you, only to discover you. You can't disappoint me."

Mary Haskell to Kahlil Gibran
November 23, 1912

Are you aware of the labels that are put on your child? Do you do it yourself? Does your child understand what the label means and act accordingly or does he seem confused by it?

Understand the Uses and Dangers of Labels
Accept Your Child As He Is
Seek a Unique Plan for Your Child's Education

Understand the Uses and Dangers of Labels

Labeling children is a widespread practice that has a potential for harm. Any label is limiting. Society does it, schools do it, peer groups do it, and worst of all, families do it to their own children. People, instead of accepting each other as unique and worthy of love and respect, express their limited expectations in the form of labels.

"This is Joe, he's our <u>athlete</u>, and Sally, she's our <u>genius</u>."

"This is Lou, she's the <u>messy one</u>, just like her father."

"Jon is our <u>lawyer</u>, he's going to follow in his uncle's footsteps."

"Mary's no <u>brain</u>, she works hard for her A's."

"Danny never cracks a book. He's just <u>naturally smart</u>."

"Jane is like I am, a <u>math dunce</u>."

Labels adhere and for better or worse have a long-lasting affect on children's lives. They have the capacity to limit your child's potential development.

Even though labeling children is a very poor practice and is not necessary, most school systems do it. Schools require that children be labeled to make them eligible for special programs designed to meet their learning needs. The programs are valuable, but the labels are not. Ideally, the school should be permitted, without labels, to develop a unique educational plan for your child, the result of an agreement among you, the teacher and your child. It should specify how his needs for the coming year will be met. Every child could benefit from this, but, at present, only children with a handicap label receive such a plan.

A Special Case: The Handicap Label

The labels schools use can have positive or negative connotations in people's minds. Labels applied to handicapped children are often explicitly negative, and they rarely describe what the individual child is capable of doing. Examples are: communication-handicapped, perceptually impaired or neurologically impaired, socially maladjusted, emotionally disturbed, mentally retarded, multiply handicapped, visually handicapped, orthopedically handicapped and preschool handicapped. Many of these labels are medical terms and have little to do with schools.

At the present time, you may not be able to eliminate the handicap label if you want your child to receive the program he needs, is entitled to and should have. You might want to make the school know your opposition to the label, however. Let them know that you would prefer that he be put into the proper program according to his unique needs and not according to the label he has been given which does not and cannot accurately describe him.

When a label is attached to your child, it is a description of an abstract group and does not adequately describe your child or his needs in concrete, behavioral terms. Most people, however, think they know what these abstractions mean and attribute certain characteristics to a child bearing these labels. This can negatively affect the child's view of himself and his ability to learn.

Common Labels Used To Characterize Children

problem child	poor attitude
lazy	hyperactive
dull	stupid
uncooperative	inattentive
slow learner	withdrawn
star pupil	aggressive
underachieving	overachieving

When you know or suspect that labels are being applied by the school, take action immediately. Ask that your child's behavior be described objectively, and that all labels be eliminated from the school's vocabulary in dealing with your child.

Labels like gifted and talented, brilliant, and genius, which designate some kind of superiority may be just as harmful to your child as labels with negative connotations. Such labels single out a child as special, whereas he may not really feel he is special. As a result, he may fear being exposed and being demoted to a less favorable position. He may conclude that it is best to keep very quiet and take no risks which could jeopardize his position. A flattering label based on one triumph may leave him unsure of what to do for an encore. Exalted status resulting from something he regards as trivial may shake his confidence in people's judgment, or teach him that his best efforts are not required in order to be labeled special.

Accept Your Child As He Is

Do not lose faith in your child if he does not score high on tests and is not labeled "superior." Creative children are not necessarily identified by these tests. Some excel on tests because they have learned the lessons in the textbook. Other equally talented children do less well on tests because they see the problem in a different, perhaps more creative way, which does not yield the textbook answer. The maverick thinker is often unacknowledged by schools especially if only textbook answers receive the "A".

Most children who act creatively continue to do so whether or not the school's program encourages it. You can help your child most by not thwarting him. Provide him with the materials, time and space he needs to carry out his projects. For this type of child do not ask, "Did you get all the answers right in school today?" Instead, inquire, "What questions did you ask today?" A creative child will appreciate the distinction instantly. Have faith in your child as a learner and he will not disappoint you.

Seek a Unique Plan for Your Child's Education

Each child should be treated uniquely. Equal opportunity demands that each child be provided with the best program that can be devised for his unique educational needs. Teachers usually know the needs of their students. The problem is lack of resources to provide for these needs. You also know your child's needs. You should encourage your school and the agencies which support it to find the resources to meet those needs by providing the necessary programs for all children without the requirement of labeling.

Chapter 9

Problem Solving

"Too often we give children answers to remember rather than problems to solve."

Roger Lewin

School, like most institutions, is not problem-free. Your child or his teacher may bring problems to your attention. Many of these present opportunities for your child to learn problem-solving skills. A few may require your intervention.

Problem-Solving Techniques
When and How To Intervene

Problem-Solving Techniques

Most of the problems which children face can and should be solved by the children themselves. You are most helpful when you teach and model good problem-solving behavior for your child. In the long run, this may be the most important tool you give him. Its development cannot be left to chance and it is **never** acquired by children whose parents solve all of their problems for them.

The first thing to do is to avoid closed responses which cut off communication. If your child says, "I hate school, and Johnny keeps pushing me." Do not respond by saying: "Don't worry, it's only the first week, next week will be better." This type of response does not help the child solve his problem and he may never confide in you again. Instead follow the steps of problem solving.

Begin by encouraging him to explore alternatives rather than giving specific advice. First clarify how your child feels about the situation: "How does it make you feel when Johnny pushes you?" It may be that your child is not angry but is sad because Johnny is the most popular boy in the class, and he wants him for a friend. You will not know this unless you ask. The next step is to help your child explore alternatives and decide what options are available to him to solve his problem. You might say: "Shall we think of some things you could do to make Johnny stop pushing you?" Try to get several ideas from your child and help him evaluate the possible outcomes of each plan. Have your child choose one idea as a course of action to pursue.

Some examples of courses of action might be: he could tell Johnny to stop it and let him know it makes him angry or sad; he could stop playing with Johnny; he could ask the teacher to change his seat; he could try to make friends by inviting Johnny to play after school at his house. After your child is committed to a course of action, let him try it and a week later, ask him how the plan is working. If the problem is not resolved to your child's satisfaction, he might want to explore another alternative. This may take more time than *your* simply stepping in and solving the problem to *your* satisfaction. It is time well spent, however, if it helps your child become an independent and creative problem solver. The child can develop a repertoire of skills so that he can successfully solve most problems he will face. Learning how to solve problems and to make decisions is as important as academic learning.

A fourth grade teacher once asked me to speak to a boy in his class because he seemed very upset and the teacher did not know how to help him. He was a good student, related well to his peers and was an asset to the group. After some questioning, the problem turned out to be that the boy and his younger brother were to be taken to a museum in New York City as a treat by the after-school program they attended. The boy felt responsible for his brother and was in a panic because he was afraid they would get lost in the museum. We tried some problem-solving techniques. First of all, we thought of the worst possible scenario. He would lose the group in the museum. What could he do if this happened? He could talk to the leader of the group and decide ahead of time where they would meet if they got lost. They could walk through this procedure to be sure everyone understood exactly where he would be. What if they still could not find him? He could call his mother in Princeton. Does he know his mother's phone number at work? He did not but he would find it out. What if he lost his money and could not use the pay phone? We then went down the hall to the pay phone and went through the procedure he could use to get the number without paying. Together, we thought of everything which could go wrong on the trip and constructed a strategy to deal with it. By the time he left, he felt much more sure of himself and seemed to be looking forward to the trip. Up until that time, he was ready to cancel the whole thing because he could think of no way to solve his problem and did not ask for help. I mention this because he was one of the brightest boys in the class academically but had not learned to use his intelligence to be a problem-solver.

When and How To Intervene

There are some problems that your child cannot solve and you may need to intervene on his behalf. When attempting to solve these problems, you can use the same problem-solving techniques you taught your child.

If your child is being physically abused, take action immediately. Make sure that the school understands that it is unacceptable. Start with the teacher. The problem should cease immediately. If not, take it to the principal. (This does not include normal confrontations with his peers which he can and should resolve himself.)

Some school systems still permit corporal punishment. If yours does, oppose it. Inform the administration immediately that you do not believe in corporal punishment and that it is not to be used on your child. It goes without saying that you should not use it as a way of disciplining your child. Physical punishment does not help a child alter his behavior, and it can destroy the parent-child relationship. You should be your child's confidant, not his adversary.

If your child is not making progress in school academically, first check for any physical problems, especially hearing or vision. A Central Auditory Test Battery may be in order. If he has auditory processing or vision problems, his program should be adjusted accordingly. If there is no physical basis for his lack of progress, request diagnostic testing in order that a more appropriate program can be put in place. Go through channels—teacher, principal and up to the superintendent if necessary.

If your child is friendless, lonely and unhappy for an extended period of time, and if problem-solving efforts have been ineffective, you may need to explore the possibility of professional help for him.

As you monitor your child's program be sure to give the teacher and school positive feedback and encouragement for their successes. If your child comes home from school excited about a new cooperative learning lesson, write a note to the teacher, with a copy to the principal and school board telling them how pleased you are with their program. If your child comes home with an innovative homework assignment or project that shows the teacher is tapping into critical thinking skills, write another note or better still, go to a school board meeting and tell the board how pleased you are. As with children, it is much more constructive to highlight the teacher's strong points rather than her deficiencies. Also, you will be viewed by the system as someone who is trying to help, not to harm.

When you do want to make a point about something which you think should be changed, put your request in the form of an "I" statement. These statements tell how you feel and how what is happening affects you. "You" statements, on the other hand, tend to place blame and make people angry. Instead of saying to a teacher, "You give too many workbook assignments and my son is not learning anything new." you might say: "I have a problem with my son doing workbook pages because I feel he does not learn as well by that method as he does by discussing the topic with peers."

Suppose you conclude that the school is seriously deficient in some respect. What should you do? First of all, assume that school officials have good intentions, and that, with proper feedback, they will make the necessary changes. Talk to the teacher first and, when appropriate, the school principal. Your attitude should be constructive. Give positive suggestions. Better yet, be willing to give some of your own time and effort to help.

If the school is unwilling to respond, or lacks the resources to do so, you may want to talk to the superintendent of schools. If this fails, try the school board. In extreme cases, it may be necessary to form a citizens committee to confront the problem. If none of your fellow citizens share your view, then you may need to seek another educational alternative for your child.

Chapter 10

Judging a School System

"We thought, because we had power, we had wisdom."
Stephen Vincent Benet

In some school systems, parents can choose which school their child will attend. These parents need to know what a good school looks like to choose wisely for their child. Even if a choice is not presently available, you should be prepared in case you are given the opportunity in the future. In the meantime, you may need to take steps to improve the environment for learning in your child's present school.

How Does The School Building Look?
Does The School's Atmosphere Encourage Learning?
Do Teachers Use A Variety Of Techniques?
Is Cooperative Learning Used?
Do People In The School Act As Positive Role Models?
Are Parents Involved In School Activities?

How Does The School Building Look?

The way to start judging a school system is to take a walk through the building on a day the school is in session. The saying: "First impressions are lasting" applies to this situation.

The first thing to notice is the building itself. Observe how the building is maintained. A well-maintained old building is more desirable than a poorly-maintained new building because it usually indicates a better school system. Clean, shining buildings and dirty, poorly maintained buildings reveal volumes about the school, not only how the students feel about their school, but also how the custodians feel about their jobs. Students who are angry and frustrated take out this anger by writing on bathroom walls and destroying property. Custodians who do not feel encouraged, appreciated or recognized by supervisors and school boards take out their feelings by doing only the minimum maintenance. A poorly maintained building negatively affects all who must use it. Students get the message that they are not very important to the adults in the school.

After you notice how well the school is maintained look to see how well space is used. Is it used flexibly? Both small and large rooms should be available to accommodate a variety of activities. Classrooms should be pleasant, preferably opening out to courtyards and the outdoors. Is there a media center and library equally accessible to all the teachers and children, and is it used? In general, is the building being used in such a way that you know everyone is actively involved in the serious endeavor of educating children with joy? Or, does the use of space give you the feeling of gloom and imprisonment in a place where learning is not as important as control?

Does The School Atmosphere Encourage Learning?

Seek an opportunity to visit a classroom and learn the answers to two sets of questions:

Do the students sit most of the time at desks regimented in orderly rows? Is the teacher always at the front lecturing at the students? Are the students prohibited from talking to each other—ever? Are pencil and paper the only tools employed?

Do the students collect in several smaller groups in different parts of the room working on different tasks? Does the teacher circulate among groups? Do the children communicate with each other within the groups? Do the students work with concrete objects and tools?

These are just two ways to run a classroom, but they are not the only ways, and neither may be the best way for your child. In order to explore the full range of classroom styles, you should visit other classrooms in your district and in other school districts.

Look to see how many children are sitting outside of the principal's office for punishment. Teachers occasionally need to send a disruptive student to a "time-out" place for their mutual benefit. However, when students are consistently sent by teachers to sit outside of the principal's office as punishment, it is time for parents to take notice. Of course, the person really being punished is the secretary who not only has to do her work, but also has to supervise the "culprits". Schools which use punitive measures to force children to behave are to be avoided. Disruptive children are discouraged and need help, not public punishment. This may be an indication that this school is not an encouraging place for children.

Listen for constant announcements on the loudspeaker. These can run the gamut from giving the names of students who are the best athletes, to getting the attendance count, to a general announcement paging the principal. Too many announcement give the message that learning in the classroom is not a high priority because anything can interrupt it.

Another thing to notice is how often students are called out of classes for such things as meetings, assemblies, picture taking and so on. A certain amount of this is necessary, but some schools let these kinds of activities take precedence over what the teacher is doing in the classroom.

What will finally make the difference for your child, however, is how he will function with that particular group of children in that particular class with that particular teacher that particular year. When the total atmosphere is encouraging for everybody in the school, your child's chances of consistently having a good teacher and a group of learners in his class increases but is not guaranteed. Asking another parent how his child did in a particular class the year before is not especially useful because your child is unique and his experience will be different from every other child's. You need to monitor his program and progress continuously. You would do that if your child were under a doctor's care no matter how great a reputation the hospital had. Do the same for your child in school.

Do Teachers Use A Variety Of Techniques?

Notice if the teachers have a repertoire of skills to accommodate the variety of learning styles found in every class. Some school systems impose the latest "innovative" program on the whole school with little input from the teachers. Some teachers respond to the new program by slavishly following its manual whether or not it fits the needs of students in their classes. Others respond by adapting the new program to fit the individual learning styles of their students.

If your child is in a new, innovative program, and he is not learning, request that the program be adapted to fit his learning style.

Good school systems encourage teachers to be flexible no matter what the program. They also train and encourage their teachers to use cooperative learning techniques as part of their repertoire.

Is Cooperative Learning Used?

The essence of cooperative learning is assigning a group goal. The teacher sets the task. The group is told the criteria that will be used to evaluate the results. The students in the group must be concerned with each other's learning, and each member of the group is responsible for knowing the work.

To complete assignments cooperatively, the students must interact with each other, share ideas and materials, pool their information and resources, use division of labor when appropriate, integrate each member's contribution into a group product, and help each other to learn. As a result, communication, conflict management, leadership and trust-building skills are developed in the students.

Cooperative group members realize that their actions affect others in the group. A student cannot sit back while others do all the work. A diversity of student ability in the group stimulates conversation among the students and forces them to verbalize. Teacher oversight of the groups in action allows for feedback to the group on their social behavior and performance and for assistance when necessary.

Mastery, retention, and transfer of concepts, are more readily acquired in cooperatively structured learning than in competitive or individually structured learning. This type of learning promotes higher quality and greater quantity of learning in addition to developing interpersonal skills. Cooperative learning lessons are also a more efficient use of classroom time.

Many teachers, convinced that cooperative learning is essential in the classroom, have had to counteract the myth that we live in a competitive world of survival of the fittest. Research has shown the opposite to be true. Hundreds of studies confirm the superiority of cooperative relationships in promoting healthy social development.

Do People In The School Act As Good Role Models?

Notice if all adults in a school act responsibly in order to be good role models for the children. If the bus driver is rude to children, and uses inappropriate language in speaking to them, then children learn that this is the way adults talk. If the cafeteria workers do not keep the cafeteria clean and pleasant, are rude to children and rush them unnecessarily through lunch, then children learn that their needs are not very important. If the secretary speaks harshly to the children and does not take time to listen to their legitimate problems, then the children learn that they and their problems are not considered important.

Opportunities for positive learning experiences are lost in these ways. Sometimes you forget that children come in contact with many adults besides the teacher in a school system. All of these adults are important in children's lives and have the potential for a positive or negative influence on them. The non-instructional members of the school community should be as adequately paid, and as carefully selected and trained as the teachers and administrators. They must know how to interact with children constructively.

Notice if staff and students speak to and about one another respectfully. Do they address each other by name as they meet in the halls and engage in the activities of the day? When students move about the halls, do they show concern for the rights of others? Is there a spirit of cooperation and respect? Or do adults cluster together in the halls ignoring the children's needs?

When you look at the school, you should see a place where everybody feels and acts encouraged. That includes custodians, cafeteria workers, aides, secretaries, students, parents, teachers, principals, superintendent and school board. They all need to feel that they are important and necessary to the smooth functioning of the school. They are all models for children, and many of the positive attributes we want our children to learn are "caught", not taught. Children are very observant and will emulate the adult models around them. A school is not a corporation with a hierarchy of power, rather it is a community of people, one of whose goals is to develop citizens who will have basic skills, who know how to learn, who are independent thinkers and who function well in a democracy.

Be alert for problems in a school system that has recently experienced a strike. Strikes tell you a great deal about the relationship between a school board and the staff. Some boards feel that their main job is to save the community money by keeping down salaries. There is a price to paid for this: a loss of trust and cooperation between the two groups.

Are Parents Involved In School Activities?

Notice if the school encourages parents to participate in school programs. Schools which welcome parents seem to benefit considerably in many ways. Parent participation enriches the school with adults who have varied backgrounds, experience and talents. It improves the adult/child ratio. Further, it provides an opportunity for constructive communication between school and parents on a daily basis. If your school does not offer them, try to get such activities started.

If you are able, you should take advantage of any opportunities the school offers which involve you in its programs. Especially, seek to be involved in those which influence school policy. Be an advocate for school councils and other forms of site-based management.

Concluding Remarks

Once, I conducted a small, informal survey by asking the question: "What is the purpose of school?" My question yielded the following answers:

- To produce responsible citizens.
- To produce thinkers.
- To develop lifelong learners.
- To protect the dreams of children.
- To teach concern for others.
- To develop all aspects of the child.
- To teach problem-solving techniques.
- To adapt to change.
- To baby-sit children and keep them off the streets.
- To keep students out of the market place.
- To produce workers.
- To help students to pass examinations.

How would you answer this question?

There is probably no single answer, but one which I would discourage is that the purpose of school is to get children **ready** for something else. Students go to nursery school to become **ready** for kindergarten. The kindergarten program makes them **ready** for elementary school. The high school program is structured to make the students **ready** to take the Scholastic Aptitude Tests and to fill out college applications. On the application a student must be **ready** to indicate he has participated in a sport, been in some community activity, been on the student council, showed independence by working at a job, taken all Advanced Placement courses and, in general, been a super-student. In its turn, the higher education system makes students **ready** for a career. As the saying goes: Life is what happens while you are planning ahead.

Somehow we have lost the sense that schooling should be an ongoing, joyful, spontaneous, creative experience, not a punitive, painful and unproductive one.

One kindergartner said to me, "Okay, I did what you wanted me to do. I learned to read. Now can I go home?" She probably intended never again to pick up another book.

You probably cannot control whether your child will become a lifelong learner since that is a personal decision he must make. You should be taking steps, however, to prevent him from being permanently conditioned against learning. The high school dropout rates indicate that this is a real possibility for many students. You can help your child by fostering a spirit of joyful learning at home and at school.

Heed the timeless wisdom on parents and children written in *The Prophet*: Be the strong and flexible bow from which your children, as arrows, take flight into the future, masters of their lives.

Things I Have Found To Be True

- Children are concrete thinkers. They cannot figure out what is expected of them if we only tell them what they did wrong. Catch them being right.
- Children who are discouraged cannot learn. Misbehaving children are deeply discouraged and do not feel they belong.
- We cannot change anybody, we can only change ourselves,
- We are all models for the children. We cannot say, "Do as I say, not as I do". Adults who are not respectful of children, cannot expect respect from them.

- Encouragement if the prime motivator. Praise is for the successes, and only a few are entitled to it. Encouragement if for the effort and we all deserve and need it.
- Accept each child completely as he is.
- Separate the deed from the doer. Never say anything against a child's person.
- Children live up to our best and worst expectations. Never label a child.
- Use "I" statements not "you" statements. Example: Instead of "You are a thief" say ""I get upset when you take money from my purse."
- Mistakes are not failures. They are how we learn.
- Rather then saying did you get an "A" say, did you ask any good questions?
- Teaching styles should vary to accommodate different learning styles.
- We cannot make anybody learn. That is a personal decision.
- Everyone in the classroom is responsible for its successes and failures.
- Cooperative learning lessons foster group cohesiveness and teach concern and respect for others.

From the Talmud: The highest wisdom is kindness.

Nancy Devlin

*   *   *

Dr. Nancy Devlin graduated from Hunter College with a degree in English and a Masters degree in Guidance and School Counseling. She taught elementary school in New York City, and in military-dependent schools in Germany, Denmark and Japan. She earned her Ph.D. in Educational Psychology at the University of California at Berkeley. She was a psychologist for twenty-two years in the Princeton Schools. She is a licensed psychologist, a family therapist and a nationally-certified school psychologist. She is married to a Physicist and they have three sons. She has published hundreds of newspaper articles on issues of education and childrearing. At present, she has a website and blog, www.Cassandrasclassroom.com providing information on education, parenting and related topics

*   *   *